Super Simple Cartooning for Kids

Do you ever scribble pictures in the margins of your notebook?

Rosa M. Curto

BARRON'S

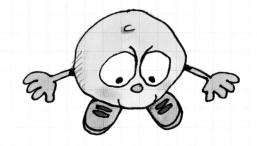

Summary

Introduction

This book is full of ideas,

exercises, and tips that will make it easy for you to create expressive comics with your own personal style. By following the instructions, watching, and practicing, you'll be surprised to see your inner creative artist come out and play. Materials you can use: paper, pencils, pens, markers, and paints.

IF YOU'RE GOOD WITH YOUR HANDS AND ARE PATIENT, YOU CAN ALSO PRACTICE MAKING COLLAGES WITH THE COMIC BOOK PANELS.

Lots of different eyes

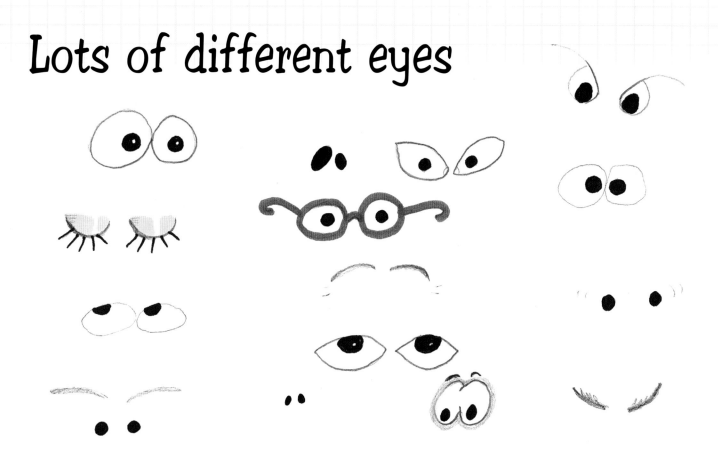

Look at all the different eyes. There are eyes with eyelashes and others with eyelids; some are round and others are almond-shaped. There are big ones and small ones.

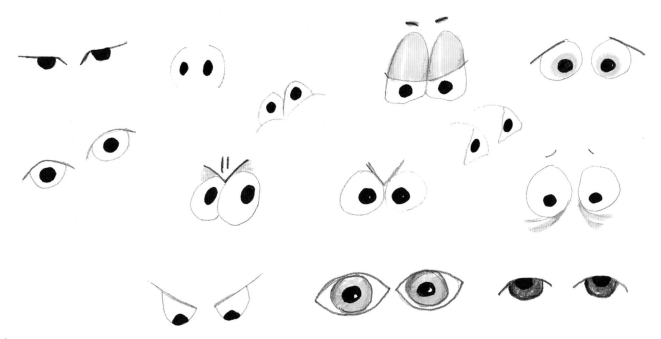

Funny faces

Draw circles and ovals on a sheet of paper.
Then draw different eyes inside your shapes.
Can you see how expressive they are?

YOU CAN ALSO BRING DIFFERENT SHAPES TO LIFE AND INVENT ALL KINDS OF WACKY EYES.

A mountain of mouths

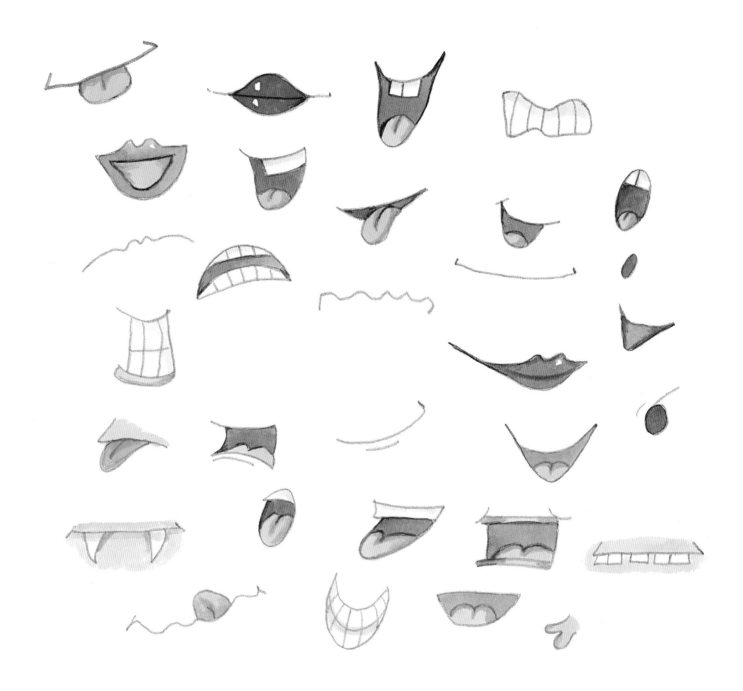

So many mouths to draw! Open, closed, baring their teeth,
sticking out their tongues...

Make-believe characters

When you make comics, you can distort reality by changing shapes and sizes. You can even invent totally fictitious characters.

HOW MANY EYES DOES THIS LITTLE MONSTER HAVE?
HOW MANY EYES ARE ON THIS PAGE?

Some very comic monsters

What do these two characters have in common?

YES, THEY'RE BOTH MONSTERS, BUT...

25

Here are ... 2 games for you

Invent characters by using some of these features.
Here's an example for you.

Copy these drawings onto a sheet of paper, and ask your friends to finish them.

YOU CAN DO IT AS MANY TIMES AS YOU LIKE.

HERE'S AN EXAMPLE.

27

Funny insects

With everything you've learned up to now, you can draw
all types of creatures easily. Practice with these four.

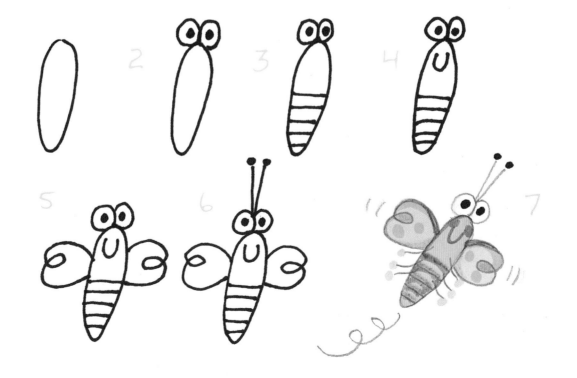

28

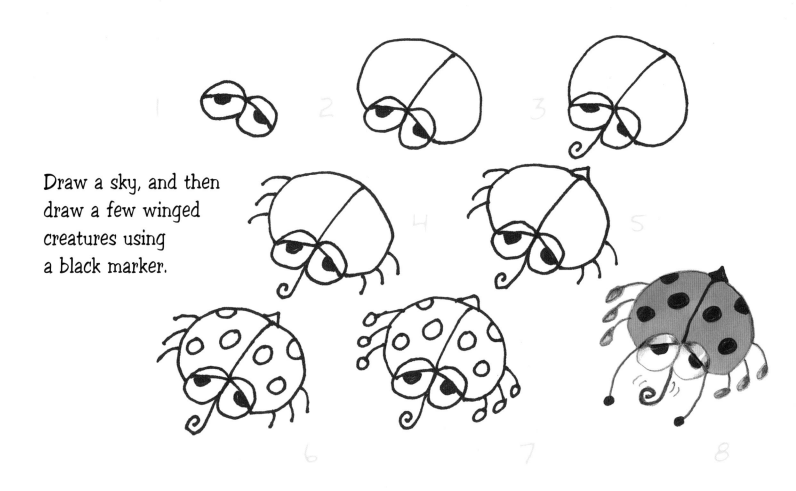

Draw a sky, and then draw a few winged creatures using a black marker.

REMEMBER THAT YOU CAN MAKE MANY DIFFERENT EYES AND MOUTHS.

Turning faces

Before starting on some new sketches, take a good look at yourself in the mirror. Move your head slowly from side to side, but always keep looking at yourself.

NOW LOOK AT THESE FACES.
THE SAME THING IS TRUE FOR PROFILES.

30

No matter how much you move,
the distance between your eyes and
nose, and between your nose and
mouth, will always be the same.

The distance from the eyes to the ears is constant,
as well as the distance from the mouth to the chin.

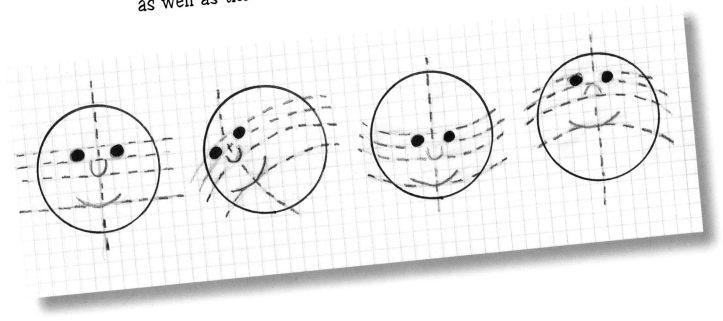

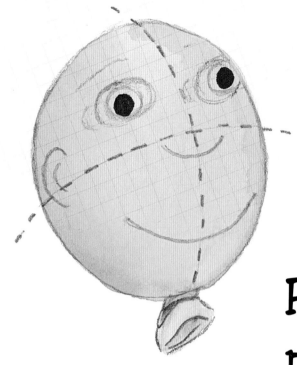

Blow up a balloon, and then draw a face on it that has eyes, a nose, a mouth, and ears. Rotate it slowly, drawing it in different positions.

Front, profile, back

Now you're going to draw a cat's head.

HAVE YOU NOTICED HOW THE DISTANCES STAY THE SAME?

To make sure you've got it, you can also try it with graph paper. Draw the cats and their bodies. Be careful with the proportions.

Now look at this owl—it's also between horizontal lines. He is shown from the front, in profile, and from the back. Note: You can draw on blank paper now. The graph paper was only to make the explanation easier to visualize.

This boy is expressing many different emotions.
Point at the happy face with your finger. Did you find it?
Now look for the angry face, the scared and worried faces,
and the dreamy face. What emotions do you think
the other faces are showing?

Expressing emotions

DRAW EMOTIONS THAT YOU HAVE FELT
ON A SHEET OF PAPER.

Make different funny faces with a friend. Pay attention
to the shape of the eyebrows, the curve of the lips,
and the opening of the eyes.

Hands also speak

Did you know that hands are also very expressive?
They give, caress, squeeze, grab, let go, press...

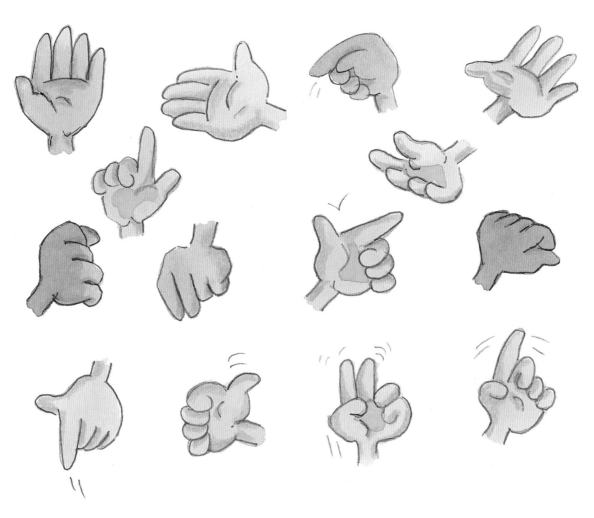

Look closely at the position of your hands.
- Grab a spoon.
- Point at the window.
- Comb your hair.
- Wave goodbye.
- Shake someone's hand.
- Drink water.

Look at the hands on this page. Copy some
of them onto a sheet of paper.

THERE ARE SOME COMIC BOOK ARTISTS WHO CREATE
HANDS WITH FOUR FINGERS INSTEAD OF FIVE.

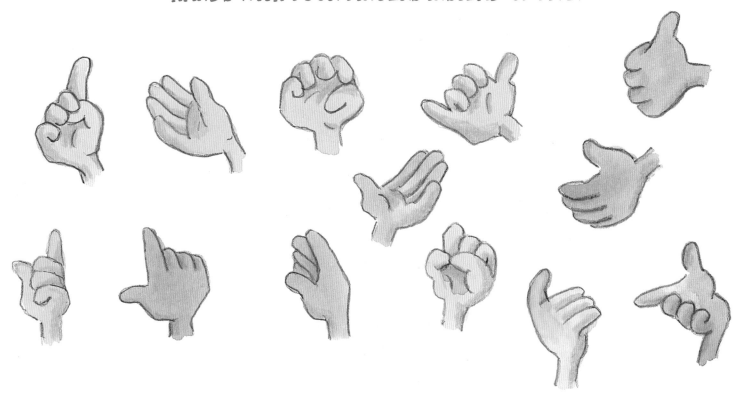

Lots of feet

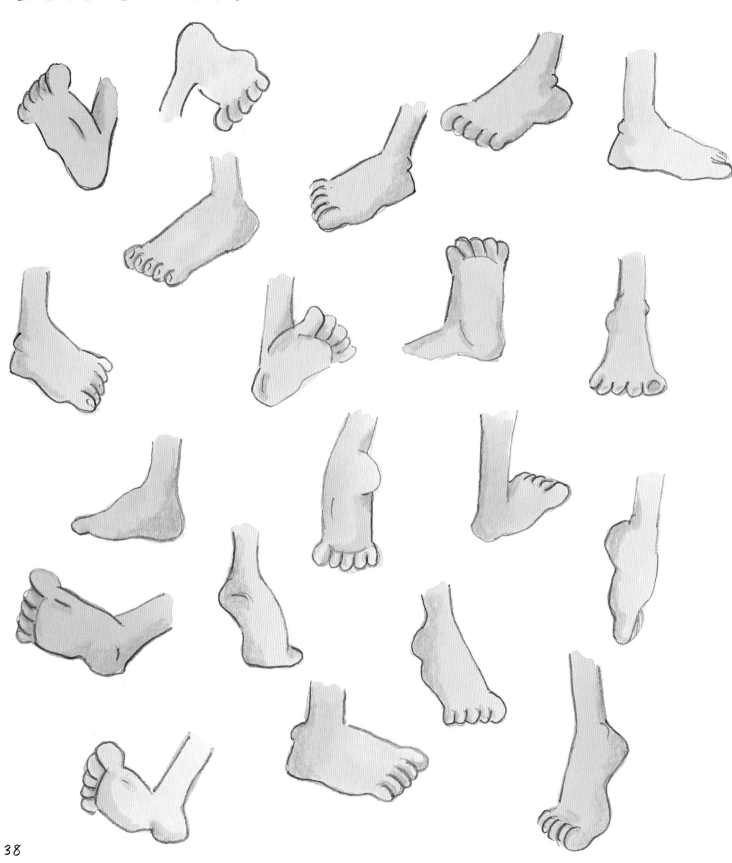

Have you ever really looked at your feet?
Study your soles, sides, ankles, and the length of your toes.
Gently massage your feet to learn their curves and shape.
Walk on your heels. Spin in circles... Play and learn!
Here are a bunch of feet. Copy some of them and draw
them with shoes, boots, or socks.

YOU CAN SIMPLIFY THE SHAPE OF THE FEET
TO MAKE IT EASIER.

With just four features, you have a character—
a simple one, but it's full of movement.

First body movements

We recommend that the elbows and knees are bent and that the head keeps turning in different positions.

Draw a boy like this one and play around with giving him movement.

Your first drawings may not turn out like you imagined them.

DON'T WORRY! JUST KEEP ON TRYING.

Playing with geometric shapes

Use different sizes and colors of stickers.

Have fun creating your own characters.

IT'S IMPORTANT TO GIVE YOUR CHARACTERS A SENSE
OF MOVEMENT, EVEN IF THEY ARE VERY SIMPLE.

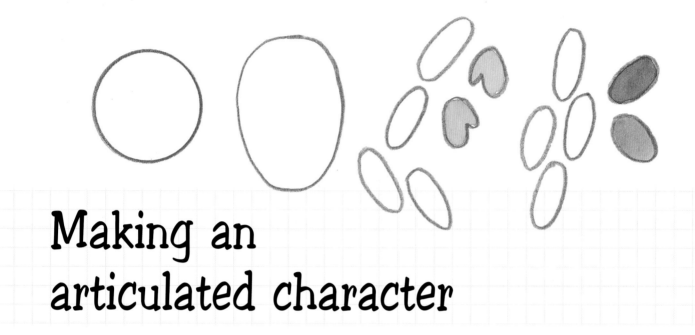

Making an
articulated character

Using a circle to make the head, an oval shape for the body, four shapes for the arms, two hands, four shapes for the legs, and two feet, you're going to make a three-dimensional boy.

CUT THESE SHAPES OUT
FROM CONSTRUCTION PAPER.

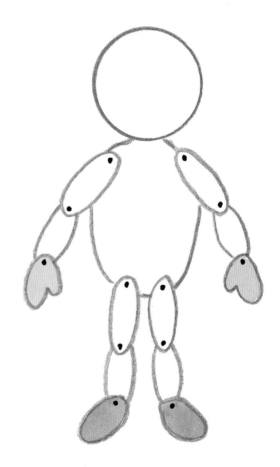

Move the pieces
to bring your
character to life.
Now draw him on
a sheet of paper.

45

Flowers come to life

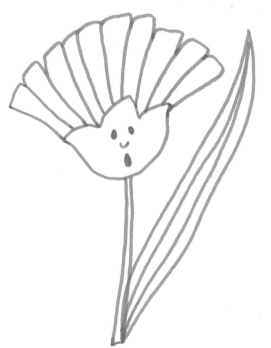

If I asked you what these images are, I'm sure you would tell me: "FLOWERS!" Although they're animated with faces, you can identify them because they have certain features: petals, stems, and leaves.

If you put them together and look for expressions,
you can even imagine they're talking to you. What do you
think they're saying?

DRAW A FLOWER WITH A FUNNY
EXPRESSION, LIKE IT IS TALKING.

A lemon

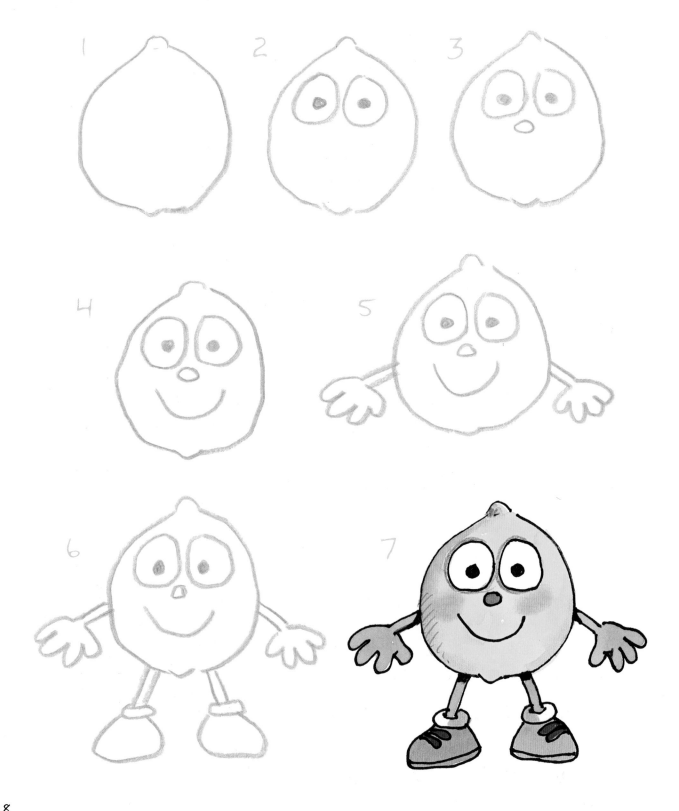

You're going to draw a lemon step-by-step and then try to add movement. Did you notice the drawings below are all the same character? Using a nonpermanent marker, draw a face on a lemon.

HOLD IT IN DIFFERENT POSITIONS AND THEN DRAW WHAT YOU SEE.

Now you're going to draw an apple
step-by-step and add movement.

An apple

Draw a few apples on a sheet of paper and create different expressions. Try changing the color and the position of each one. Be inventive!

WHICH DO YOU LIKE THE BEST? WHY? ARE THEY ALL THE SAME CHARACTER?

A star

Let's draw a star with five points step-by-step. Look for new expressions and movements. Use your imagination.

DON'T WORRY ABOUT COLORING IT WHILE YOU'RE PRACTICING.

Falling leaves

Cut out several leaves.
Draw the outline on white
construction paper.

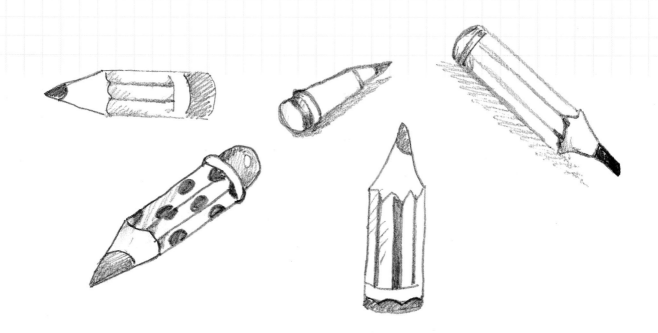

Put colored pencils of different sizes and thicknesses on a table. Study them.

Smiling pencils

Take one and look closely at it: straight, at an angle, on its side...

Now, draw a few pencils in different positions, and then animate them and color them in.

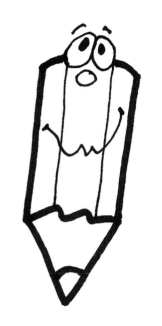

If you change the face and color of a pencil, you'll have a whole new character.

YOU CAN EVEN PUT A HAT OR OTHER ACCESSORIES ON IT.

YOU ARE NOW DRAWING COMICS!

Animating inanimate objects

Pick several
inanimate objects
that you see
around you.

DRAW THEM ON BLANK PAPER,
ANIMATE THEM, AND COLOR THEM IN.

What face would you draw on this cracker with a bite out of
it? Happy, sad, surprised, angry? What about the paintbrush?
What expression do you think the fork would have
if you drew it loaded up with spaghetti?

Breaking stereotypes

Imagine you have a pen or pencil in your hand, and draw it without thinking too much. You'll discover you suddenly have a character and you'll want to give it a personality.

You already have the shape; now you can play around with colors. How about orange and brown legs?

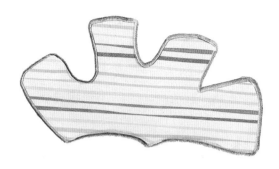

Maybe spiky hair?

Draw a rooster and color it so it is UNIQUE.

COLOR HELPS YOU CHARACTERIZE YOUR CHARACTERS.

Graphic symbols

Images have a lot of strength in the world of comics.
They are accompanied by symbols and lines that strengthen
the characters' actions and emotions.

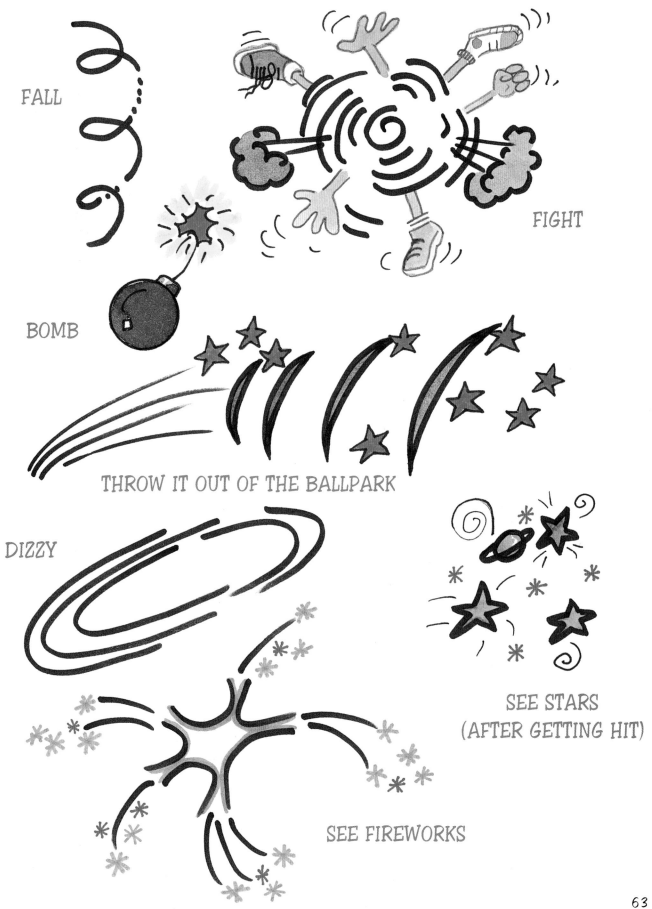

FALL

FIGHT

BOMB

THROW IT OUT OF THE BALLPARK

DIZZY

SEE STARS
(AFTER GETTING HIT)

SEE FIREWORKS

SPLASH

BOOM

Symbols with text

Decorated letters also add visual language fast.
They are another tool for expression.

DEFLATE

SNAP YOUR FINGERS

THE PHONE

JUMP

THUNDER &
LIGHTNING

BLUSH

GRRR!...

ANGER

LAUGHTER

Characters and symbols

Look at these illustrations.
Explain each situation.
Draw a character to give
expression to: "Grrr!"

We will now show you how to make a turtle.
Draw some of these turtles but change their
colors, eyes, and positions.

Turtles

GIVE THEM YOUR PERSONAL TOUCH!

Rabbits

Now we'll show you how to make a rabbit.
Draw rabbits and personalize them however you like!
Try exaggerating the shapes: shorter or thicker legs, huge eyes...

Squirrels

Here are a bunch of squirrels as examples.
Pick two or three and draw them as if they were talking
to each other. You don't need to write anything.

Cats

On a blank piece of paper, draw the cat step-by-step.
Add the letter "z" to show that she's sleeping.

EXPLAIN TO SOMEONE WHAT THE OTHER CATS
ARE THINKING OR SAYING.

All of these dogs are drawn with lines around them.
Look at them! What does each line move?
Draw a dog and add lines to make him move.

Dogs

Elephants

Draw the elephant following the steps below, but change the colors. Look at the elephants on the right-hand page.

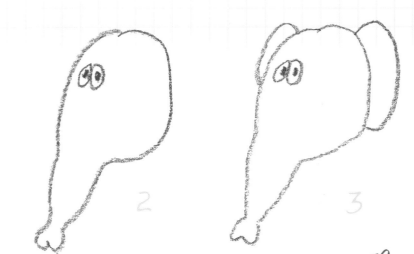

WHICH ONE DO YOU THINK IS THE FUNNIEST? WHY?

Create your own elephant. Remember, you can change it and add lines to show movement.

Bears

Draw the bear step-by-step. Color it in and decorate
it however you like!
Pick one of these bears and draw it with an elephant
and a turtle.

Duck and baby goat

Look at the duck and the baby goat.
We drew them first on graph paper and then on blank
paper. Invent one and try drawing it in different positions.

ALL CHARACTERS LOOK
LARGER WHEN THEY
ARE CLOSER TO US AND
SMALLER WHEN THEY ARE
FARTHER AWAY.

A world of emotions and movements

Look at all these funny characters, and then look closely at how the lines and symbols on each one expresses emotions and feelings and movement. If you learn the language of comics, you often won't need words.

STARE

SHOCKED

DIZZY

BLUSH

ABSENT-MINDED

SHAKE YOUR HEAD

SLIP

FALL DOWN

ANGRY

FALL FROM
REALLY HIGH

SCARED

WORRIED

WALK FAST

Creating a unique character

These two pages contain a jumble of different shapes.
On a sheet of blank paper, play and invent animals using these
shapes. Strengthen their actions by drawing lines and symbols.

You can change
colors and repeat the
shapes as many times
as you want.

LOOK AT THE EXAMPLE.

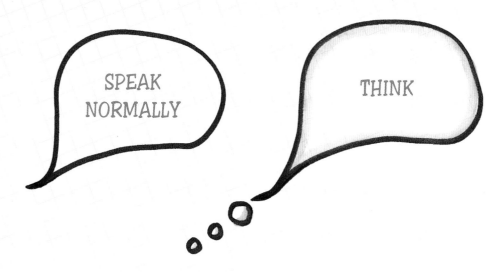

Expressive balloons

Text in comic books is normally placed inside balloons.
You can express their emotions by changing their shapes.

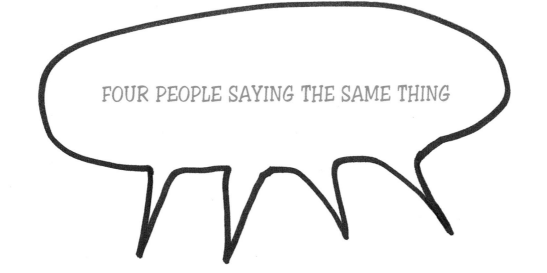

Balloons with symbols

Some symbols are also depicted inside balloons or in the panel.

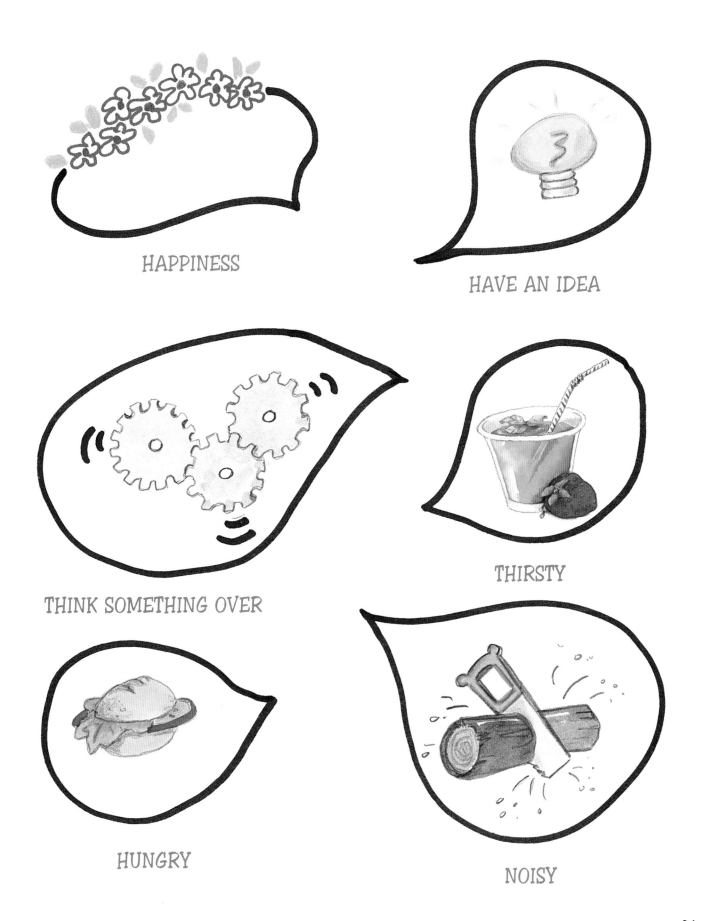

HAPPINESS

HAVE AN IDEA

THINK SOMETHING OVER

THIRSTY

HUNGRY

NOISY

Laying out comic book panels

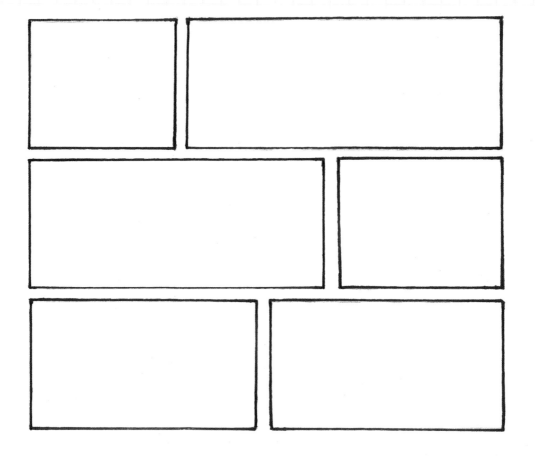

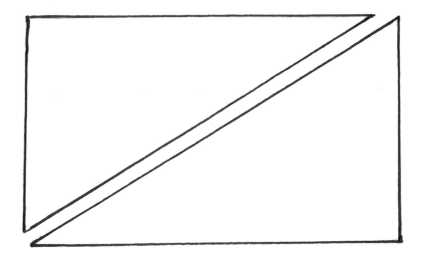

The layout changes depending on the story
you're telling, as well as the panel shapes.

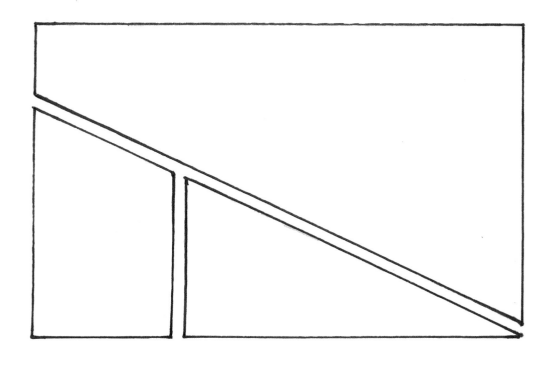

The image is the most important thing in comics.
You tell stories by making a series of drawings.
You've seen how characters can be simple, but they
must be expressive.

Words aren't always necessary

NOW YOU ARE READY TO TELL YOUR OWN STORIES. DRAW COMIC PANELS WITH YOUR OWN PERSONAL STYLE!

First edition for North America published in 2016
by Barron's Educational Series, Inc.
ISBN: 978-1-4380-0826-4

© GEMSER PUBLICATIONS, S.L. 2015
El Castell, 38   08329 Teià (Barcelona, Spain)
www.mercedesros.com
Text and illustrations: ROSA M. CURTO
Design and layout: ESTUDI GUASCH, S.L.

Printed in China
9 8 7 6 5 4 3

Date of Manufacture:
April 2018
Manufactured by:
L. Rex Printing Company
Limited, Dongguan, China

All inquiries should be addressed to:
Barron's Educational Series, Inc.
250 Wireless Boulevard
Hauppauge, NY 11788
www.barronseduc.com